NOW AND FOR A TIME

John Fuller

Chatto & Windus
LONDON

Published by Chatto & Windus 2002

2 4 6 8 10 9 7 5 3 1

Copyright © John Fuller 2002

John Fuller has asserted his right under the Copyright, Designs
and Patents Act 1988 to be identified as the author of this work

First published in Great Britain in 2002 by
Chatto & Windus
Random House, 20 Vauxhall Bridge Road,
London SW1V 2SA

Random House Australia (Pty) Limited
20 Alfred Street, Milsons Point, Sydney,
New South Wales 2061, Australia

Random House New Zealand Limited
18 Poland Road, Glenfield,
Auckland 10, New Zealand

Random House (Pty) Limited
Endulini, 5A Jubilee Road, Parktown 2193, South Africa

The Random House Group Limited Reg. No. 954009
www.randomhouse.co.uk

A CIP catalogue record for this book
is available from the British Library

ISBN 0 7011 7351 3

Papers used by Random House are natural,
recyclable products made from wood grown in sustainable forests;
the manufacturing processes conform to the environmental
regulations of the country of origin

Typeset by Deltatype Limited, Birkenhead, Merseyside

Printed and bound in Great Britain by
Mackays of Chatham plc

ACKNOWLEDGEMENTS

Grateful acknowledgements are made to the following, in which some of these poems first appeared: *52nd Aldeburgh Festival of Music and the Arts Programme Book, Clutag Poetry Leaflet no. 2, The Mind has Mountains, Oxford Magazine, Oxford Poetry, Poetry Ireland, Poetry Review, Tertulian Poems, Thumbscrew, Times Literary Supplement.*

CONTENTS

BIRTH BELLS FOR LOUISA

1

The awaited moment is almost with us,
Beneath the leaves we look and listen,
    Now and for a time.

The present is here and what comes after?
Nestlings are noisy in the creeper's shadow,
    Now and for a time.

Beneath the leaves we look and listen.
Summer is spending its songs within,
    Now and for a time.

Nestlings are noisy in the creeper's shadow.
Just for a season the blackbird is master,
    Now and for a time.

Summer is spending its songs within.
It seems that the music will never be finished,
    Now and for a time.

Just for a season the blackbird is master.
Hope is attendant like an arrow,
    Now and for a time.

It seems that the music will never be finished,
The awaited moment is almost with us
    Now and for a long time.

2

When the sky bruises and rain runs silver,
What better to receive it than a river?
    The mirror keeps your face.

Clouds passing, with curtains attached,
The surface dimpled, the water a ladder.
>   The mirror keeps your face.

What better to receive it than a river,
The glad bounce and joy of liquid?
>   The mirror keeps your face.

The surface dimpled, the water a ladder,
Giving always and therefore taking.
>   The mirror keeps your face.

The glad bounce and joy of liquid,
All energy passing into stillness.
>   The mirror keeps your face.

Giving always and therefore taking,
As wandering comes to its harbour.
>   The mirror keeps your face.

All energy passing into stillness,
When the sky bruises and the rain runs silver.
>   The mirror keeps your face for ever.

3

Sounds of the summer surprise in silence,
Water in movement beneath the light,
>   Listening for a cry.

Strokes of tennis like chalk breaking,
The river sparkling on the weir,
>   Listening for a cry.

Water in movement beneath the light
Never pausing, parting for islands,
>   Listening for a cry.

The river sparkling on the weir,
Replenishing as it races away,
  Listening for a cry.

Never pausing, parting for islands
Where a new life begins its living,
  Listening for a cry.

Replenishing as it races away,
Ears attuned to the world's playing,
  Listening for a cry.

Where a new life begins its living,
Sounds of the summer surprise in silence,
  Listening for a strange cry.

4

Fruit falls when the fruit is ready.
Watch as you will, you'll never time it,
  The summer speeds.

Raspberries tumbling from the canes:
Blink in the sun and they are there.
  The summer speeds.

Watch as you will, you'll never time it,
The life that clamours for its visit.
  The summer speeds.

Blink in the sun and they are there,
The features you anticipated.
  The summer speeds.

The life that clamours for its visit
In the blood's delicate factory.
  The summer speeds.

The features you anticipated
Sing to the surrounding air.
    The summer speeds.

In the blood's delicate factory
Fruit falls when the fruit is ready,
    The summer speeds on its way.

5

Time now makes a new beginning.
The world is both outside and inside.
    Live with our love.

At this moment there is no past
And consciousness is everywhere.
    Live with our love.

The world is both outside and inside
And now the worlds must be united.
    Live with our love.

And consciousness is everywhere
Of newly integrated spaces.
    Live with our love.

And now the worlds must be united
Into a manifold of being.
    Live with our love.

Of newly integrated spaces
What shall we say except that they
    Live with our love?

Into a manifold of being
Time now makes its new beginning.
    Live with our love, with our love.

6

Play again the intense music
That he had heard before the birth:
        It is what you are.

Lift the bow that conjures air
With such mysterious vibrations.
        It is what you are.

That he had heard before the birth
Such distant sound is so, clearly:
        It is what you are.

With such mysterious vibrations
The heart is stroked into its calm.
        It is what you are.

Such distant sound is so clearly
Close, as its pulse is to your skin.
        It is what you are.

The heart is stroked into its calm
As though a bird were kept from danger.
        It is what you are.

Close as its pulse is to your skin,
Play again the intense music:
        It is what you always were.

7

Now and for a time
The mirror keeps your face.

Listening for a cry,
The summer speeds.

Live with our love.
It is what you are.

THE SEVEN ANGELS OF TIME

1

I wriggled like a cat
From the smothering arms
Of insensibility.

The first spring of my heel
Touched light from rock:
There on the heights they still worship.

When my mouth stretched open
In a delicious yawn,
All sorts of coloured shapes

Tumbled out and turned
Into a model army whose manoeuvres
Were never real battles.

But beware: everyone
In turn becomes
His own commander-in-chief.

2

I lobbed the moon
Like a snowball which smudged the sky,
And the waters followed.

Your blood reminds you of its tides.
Your gut is the Ark of Betrayal,
Shitting the creation.

Standing proud from your body
Is the Vessel of Insolence
With which you will repeople the world.

3

I began with the soil,
Where rock had been forgetful.
Who could have foreseen it?

Lie with your ear pressed
To the hot lid of the field
And you will hear the seed uncurling.

Roots creak and branches
Echo them. The eye goes upwards
And outwards.

Above the Table of Love
Is the model of the planets.
This is the holiday of the soul.

4

I imagined that night followed day
And so invented numbers.
I could believe in symmetry.

In the height of my ambition
I was able to spin into infinity
The accident of star and snowflake.

Nothing that is not created
At this moment will last.
You will never sleep so well.

In your head is a whole clear vision
Of the future: a mirror
In the shape of the world.

5

I am the dangerous one, who
With a touch of the little finger
Created the absurd heterotrophes.

After me, all plans are possible:
Illusions of independence, magnificence
Of motion, dreams of divorce.

You are sometimes tired now,
Administering rebellion.
You have suddenly realised

That you belong nowhere.
There is no further appointment.
The centre is where you are.

6

I compounded the blunder and
In a spirit of playfulness I discovered
A form that could discreate itself.

Conceiving divinity, therefore,
You can only mock it.
You have raced ahead of the light.

Nailed by the defeat
Of bone after bone, your head
Is an explosion of myths.

You pretend that the incorporeal
Might be permanent
And you reduce the Many to the One

So that you may cease trying
To look round corners and at last
Understand the unanswerable question.

7

I am perfect nothingness.
My only instructions
Are to give you a vision of the angels

Which you may take with you
As you run screaming into
The Sabbath of oblivion.

JOE'S DREAM

at the Dartington Summer School of Music

A stillness falls upon him
Though the chords strike up again.
For an hour, the world is dismissed:
Head fallen to one side
And, in repose, a fist.

Sometimes he has been these sounds,
All of them: nothing could hide it.
The lady opened the wonderful box
And he was inside it.
Her fingers touched the strings,
The strings were unsprung locks
And the sound beat up like wings.

Joe, Joe, what do you see?
The mower under the mulberry tree.
The falling mulberry, black as blood,
That leaves the tree for ever,
Alighting with a thud.

Joe, Joe, what do you hear?
Horns of the Hall, 'how thin and clear',
And distant birdsong, like a cry
To hold the summer, trickling off
The edges of the sky.

Behind his fastened eyes
The fairy of the moment
Dances her trick of memory,
An aery nothingness
That promises to stay.

From now on, nothing dies
But enters in that dance:
The bird, the mulberries;
A pair of butterflies
That tumble up the stairs
In air; the garden orchestras.

His head stirs. He sighs.
The world is a great adventure
In which he will take his chance.
Nothing exists till he has tried it.
He wakes, and all the while
The music played, she was the music.
This is her body and her smile,
And he is outside it.

STREET LANGUAGE

1 Pigeons in Balham High Road

This is what you wanted, and what you lean
Out to see from your pushchair: the pigeons
Hunched in the feathered ruffs of their grey greatcoats.

What is it you find to say about these old soldiers?
Is it the startling rise and flutter of broken wings
Above their waddling interest in scraps, the stoical hoarding

And release of rivalrous impulses, that intrigues you?
They are not beautiful, these exiles, but they strike
The attitudes still of their feathered and aerial kind.

Simply they are pavement birds, of the gutter
And fending life. Their memory of exploit
Is like your intuition of its possibility.

For you murmur over their names in your own way,
Your own babble and cooing, that knows what it is
To be so privileged in life as to have such a great idea of it.

2 Fuchsia

What does the flower say, which you have learned to touch
Without tearing, cupping it briefly beneath the chin?
Its bright lips seem to open in wonder, like your own.

You are held up to it, as to the light of a lantern,
And light is all it needs, the adjectival voice of colour,
Repetitive, exclamatory, and at the same time silent.

The garden is red at the ends, as though it had been dipped,
Red and magenta, like the bells of a jester.
It bursts into its still and soundless frenzy.

In this fragrant room without a ceiling, water is trickling
And you are eager again to strangle the green snake.
Yours will be the human language of busy verbs.

The grass is crawling with its own little phrases of wings and
    legs.
The air is full of the flag telegraphy of butterflies.
What does the flower say? Bffzz-tszz-zng-btzzzzz . . .

3 Da

What will the first word be, Daddy or Dog?
Neither are wholly benign, like nursery Nana,
Nor wholly disgraceful, like kennelled Mr Darling.

They are both words you can hammer your tongue under.
Da, you say. Oh! Da, is what it says, too.
Da, you say. It is both a self-touching and a projection.

Like all language, you feel it between your head
And the world that rolls unendingly before you
As you chase across the rug, slapping it out of the way.

While you are crawling, you can pretend to be the dog
Who fascinates you. But surely preference must be given
To the tall Da who makes you fly? A puzzle!

Down from the ceiling, twisting to get to the rug again
To be that rough one, you briefly brush the mouth that is
    like yours.
Now, think of all the words you can say standing up.

4 Radio Baby

Beneath the eaves they are talking to their mothers
And their mothers are talking, too, with pacifying voices
Over systems of alarm that accidentally connect

Speaker to speaker, from nursery to bedroom
And from house to house, the length of Tunley Road.
What can a baby have to say to a mother who is not his
    own?

It's a busy wavelength that will blur like this,
Thinner than an eyelash darkened with tears.
It is the kinship of blood, like a year of fine wines.

But a mother knows the voiceprint of her own child,
Knows it in utter darkness, in her sleep of remembered
    maidenhood,
In the silence of communication and in the chatter of dawn.

This is Radio Baby you are tuned to, Radio Baby!
With all its regular programmes, its clatter and
    announcements.
Its easy quizzes. The laughter. The audience participation.

5 Drums at the Tooting Durbar

M'Lord's carriage has stalled in the grass, in the commons.
Shall there be dancing to entertain him?
Shall they entertain him, the dainty kings and queens?

What's this, a dog? Oh! Oh! But it's unbelievable!
The freedom, the roughness of utterance! And the colours in
    the sky.
The strolling in no direction. The sizzling sweetmeats.

What is the difference between a drum and a balloon?
A balloon is large enough to head-butt through the grass
At the pace of a controlled scamper. A drum is a sound.

The drums speak the language of a nodding procession,
Hips turning, fingers pointing, fingers fat with rings,
Whole bodies edging along, half queue, half conga.

The drums speak the language of golden crowns,
Bent knuckles on the skin, dabbling the cheeks of the drum,
The sound filling the fragrant afternoon like a fountain.

STRING QUARTET

First Violin   Loving and unloved, my true vocation
               Has been to lodge a claim on everything.
               The world is beautiful in our translation.
               It has forgotten us. Therefore I sing.

Second Violin Loved and unloving, I can only echo
               This need I almost understand (resistance
               To the dead otherness of absence), echo
               Its wonder, its tenderness and its insistence.

Viola   Loved and loving, I am outside time.
               My ear is closely bent to the unheard,
               And what I add is quiet speculation.

Cello   Unloved, unloving, savagely I must climb
               Out of self-pity. Passion is deferred.
               I am rock. I am driven. I am pure notation.

PIANO CONCERTO

Mikhail Pletnev at Angoulême

He takes the even steps of the resolute prisoner
Entering an arena of prepared discomfort.

He offers himself as for a half-portrait,
Turning slightly in the attentive light.

Do we expect speeches? He is silent.
He needs to earn our blessing still.

We have come for the confessions
That only pain can finally extort.

We want to hear the challenge of the forbidden,
The chattering of dissent, the stubbornness of heroism.

We want to hear the emotion
That belongs to the solitary truth.

We want to applaud the heretic.
We need this excuse for an old debate.

The instruments are held carefully
For they have been primed and charged.

The inquisitors look elsewhere:
Not one of them is less guilty than he is.

And now he takes his place, bowing his head.
And the instruments are raised. And it begins.

It is as we knew it might be:
The truth is not solitary, but an understanding.

Finally we know we are of neither party
But are impartial witnesses.

Out of the half-open black book of his torture
He reads the legends of joy in red and gold.

Their narrative is reflected in his cheeks and jaw
Which lift and tighten to control their uncertain hopes.

His fingers recreate the text as a river
That floods its black shores to conclusion.

There is, after all, nothing to defy.
He merely meditates upon its own laws.

Who suspected that these sublime proposals
Had once been made by authority itself?

Which now answers them in its own manner,
Turbulent, generous, bitter, enriched?

Behind his closed eyes there may be intuitions
Of which we can only appraise the translated fragments.

That his little problems in logic might have puzzled a child
Is our wonderfully encouraging conclusion.

And so they might be forgiven, as a child is forgiven,
Who then will jump and sing past bedtime.

Jump and sing until the ceiling thunders
With the moral happiness of justice done.

The noises we make in response are shouts of pure delight.
The execution was faultless.

MOSAÏQUE MACARONIQUE

Interlocking circles seek
A teasing labyrinthine plan
A travers le Basilique,
Un pavé cailloutis romane.

Galets lisses de Saint-Pierre,
Blancs et noirs, ils s'entremêlent,
And we ourselves are walking there,
Treading the shapes of Heaven and Hell.

Dim penitential voices bless
The soaring vaults with F in alt,
Mais sous les pieds de nos faiblesses
Sont cailloux polis de basalte.

Austère Mosé et Saint-Pierre
Se rencontrent en mosaïque,
Stone on stone established where
The law itself is a mystique.

A grown cathedral can be seen
As something larger than a cairn.
Ses carrés rouges comme nougatine
Coupés des volcans de l'Auvergne.

Parfois dans le Basilique
Le basilic comme hypnotiste:
Mountains are where the guilty seek
Interrogation of the Beast.

The walls delight in the grotesque;
God has a righteous chase in view.
Démembrements animent les fresques;
La voûte dévoile un Absolu.

Le samedi chez le Basilique:
Parfum de basilic, tomates.
Stalls along the pavement reek
Of all that haunts the human heart.

Every earthly thing we risk
Eternity to smell just once:
Odeur de la jeune odalisque,
Le sensualité d'encens.

LE TRAIN MALIN

This is my train song as it rattles through
Lullabaloo—lullabaloo,
The chestnut trees beneath the blue
From Corte to Aiacciu.

The cheeky little train that runs all day
Lullabaloo—lullabaloo,
Ultramarine and café-au-lait
Up to the mountain, down to the bay.

The track on its sleepers is a kind of stair
Lullabaloo—lullabaloo,
That curves and tunnels everywhere,
Depth for height, water for air.

In studious Corte all the bells sound hourly
Lullabaloo—lullabaloo,
Above the green-bronze shape of Paoli,
Dignified, but striding sourly.

They found him in the ancient citadel
Lullabaloo—lullabaloo,
They locked up Reason in a cell
And stopped the tale it had to tell.

The granite of the head must play its part
Lullabaloo—lullabaloo,
And yet the sea is where we start,
The ready motions of the heart.

The train hoots loudly as it now descends
Lullabaloo—lullabaloo,
Clearing the line, taking the bends,
Knowing that its journey ends.

Rivers are dry and pebbly in their beds
Lullabaloo—lullabaloo,
Piglets are squealing in their sheds
And the slow cyclists turn their heads.

A pair of horses standing tail to tress
Lullabaloo—lullabaloo,
Who never heard of faithlessness
Or felt they needed to impress.

And from the window what at last we see
Lullabaloo—lullabaloo,
Is nothing but the place that we,
Being not there, had wished to be.

AIGRETTE GARZETTE TO ECHASSE BLANCHE

Follow, follow, white shadow
With nowhere to go.
Row over the empty air!

I am the guardian
Of the black bulls,
Snapper of libellules!

I am appointed
To whip the bounds,
To apportion duties.

You will never reach
The vision that I have
Of the earth's ending.

You are nothing at all, a copy
Of your reflection
In the flooded fields.

A blank eye
Wearied of wandering,
Easily startled.

You want to be like me,
Sharing the stirred reeds,
The ruses of horizon.

You perch at a distance,
The beak embarrassed in feathers,
Explosions of laughter.

[. . .]

Rivers push the land into the sea,
Trickle of waters,
The lagoons ending in fire.

Ever and forever a shadow
With nowhere to go.
Row over the empty air!

MADAME FURET

Madame Furet on her whirlwind visit
    Has much to tell,
Banging at cupboards that will not open
    (Just as well),
Nosing at bags, fruit-stones, fruit-rind,
    Ends of bread,
Lifting her head to a table, diving
    Under a bed:
'When you may well in a year or two
    Be much vexed
To wonder further than the breath
    That is your next
And not impossibly your last,
    Remember me
Who live entirely at such moments,
    Free and unfree
By virtue of my breeding close
    To hopelessness,
That hedge-home where comfort has
    No known address.
I give you one brave look, as though
    You were a god
Whose only carelessness, to leave
    Crumbs where you trod,
Were too painful a puzzle for solving,
    As though square caves
Were hunger's heaven, defining the space
    In which the slaves
Of cornerless Nature are translated
    To emperors,
And the emptiness a mystery
    Daunting to us
But truly a required adventure,
    A threshold crossed
In despite of danger to my kind

And the sky lost.
But, shadowless, you do not move.
          In your eye
Is a surprise of recognition.
          Let me pass by
Before you find me quite at home.
          Be still in surprise:
Give me time to be gone
          Or otherwise
Yourself turn from our encounter.
          You will have time
To judge, with humour if you will,
          My little crime.'
Bow-legged, one wave from ear to tail,
          She scampers past
With a panic skitter on the tiles,
          Moving fast
For green and safety. And the cease of speech.

SENTINEL

At six o'clock the nameless bird we call
An egret stands sentinel upon a rock
Of indistinguishable darkness from it.
The sea moves like molten decoration,
A carpet laid before it to the sun.
The air, a medium its watchfulness
Makes startlingly clear around it,
Reflects the dwindling passage of the day.

Wings extended greet the smallest wind
That lends its texture to that graven gold
As if such gesture brought it into being,
Priestly response to the expected signs.
Its bill is pointed, head raised and alert:
This silhouette is neither flight nor dive
But shares, in stillness, such propulsiveness,
The shore beneath it wants to shake it free.

What it requires from these last hours of light,
An estimate of prey, or claim of place,
Or simply play of breeze, we do not know.
This is its chosen rock and territory.
Within this bay the cycle of its life
Turns with the sun, and it is somehow pleased
To mark another day, and stand for one
Last time before it dives into that fire.

RATATOUILLE AT VILLANOVA

Pepper, tomato, pepper and oil,
Onion, aubergine, onion and parsley,
Olive, courgette, olive and salt.

The bitterness of gourds in the richness of oil,
The ease of the heart in the savour of earth,
The openness of spirit in the fruit of the garden.

To eat on a terrace is to be welcomed back
As minor characters to the lost play of our lives,
Careless of outcome, knowing we will not change.

The sun moulds the oilcloth to the table
Like a painter casually preparing a canvas
For a study of nature he knows will make him famous.

Sea heaves its marble and sky is perfectly empty:
A sprig of dry herbs in a pot casts a shadow of ink,
And ink writes nature back into its own surface.

We are appointed to visualise a noble history
Of our latest entrance into the air,
But know it will turn out a comedy of sorts.

Come to me, my Maillol, with your salad of kisses!
Come with the ratatouille, cold from the shadow,
Bathed in its own horizon, the potter's careful thumb.

CARGHJESE

L'anachorète hélas a regagné son nid. Max Jacob

Carghjese! The lamps come on at evening
And all that we wish for through a long
Day distils to a disappearance,
To dusk and a soundless song.

A late sail makes for somewhere,
The bay as silent as a book.
It stands still at our attention,
But gets there as we look.

There is an ikon in Carghjese
By a Greek hand, which shows the night
Coiled and rebellious against
The celebrated light.

A hunched and galloping St George
Drills the Dragon in the head.
Through scrolls and arcs of golden air
The idle eye is led

Down through the lance which is directed,
With all a surgeon's swift decision,
At obvious evil, to the core
Of an intent precision.

There is a kind of darkness in
Such concentration. The mind
And these lilies lose their colour when their
Contour is defined.

Stare as we will, the sun is still
Moving too slowly for us. We
Are restless in its orange light.
It settles on the sea.

And the horizon moves through cinder,
Smoke and rose to reach that realm
Where water is the pit of stars
And the gaze drops from the helm.

Carghjese is the throb of a distant shore,
Windows of the town like a lit barque.
The solitary sun croons in his cell,
Victorious in the dark.

WORDS

for Al Alvarez at seventy

Words expended are not spent,
Like singed coloured tubes found in grass,
        Nor lost beyond call in woodland
Attended in their drowsiness by featherbreasted bedmakers
        From an attic of leaves.

Words are soldiers filing into
The narrow places of our daily distress,
        Fighting for us so fiercely
That when one falls another is ready
        To stand and be recognised.

Words are unwoundable as angels,
Flourished as banners are flourished when we
        Imagine that some futile gesture
Will keep the little scavengers from arriving
        Too early at the feast.

As Bellow said, this is
The difficulty with people who spend their
        Lives in humane studies and
Therefore imagine once cruelty has been described
        In books it is ended.

The same with mere expiry
And bodily vanishing into the unimaginable void:
        Words that have been voiced
Hover at that portal no less unwilling
        To be forgotten. Or useless.

HOW

When is when the fingers drop
From sentences that stay unread.
When is a heaviness of head.
When is the sighing that will stop.

When is the evening of a day
That darkens early, only snow,
But like a lid it lets us know
That here's a thing that will not stay.

And here's a thing, and here's a thing
That hides the when with busy how
And makes the interest of now,
The present's usual vanishing.

And here's a thing, and here's a thing:
The danger of the maze is dead
And cold the end of every thread,
And every ed no more an ing.

I'd have you follow, if you will,
Or wait, if that's the way it goes,
Suspended like the stump of rose
Or snowdrop on the window-sill.

For we may have another spring,
And now its chance to make a mark
And eyes shine brightly in the dark
And here's a thing, and here . . .

WHEN I AM DEAD

This is addressed to you
From an immaterial where,
A non-place that is nothing
But what is in your head
As my words assemble there.

I am that silent state
In which we make no choice;
Stillness holding no promise;
Darkness that is all present;
Image that has no voice.

I am a kind of fulfilment,
The last flame in a fire.
Unlike a proposition
I am both true and false.
I am what you desire.

I am a visitation,
Not the dripping ghost
Of some restless regret,
But something gladly encountered,
The thing you want the most.

I come to you in dreams
And you wake upon the kiss.
If even now we are haunted,
No wonder that we cherish
The love we already miss.

Like this, when I am dead
The words and shadows move,
Translucent as ever, candid,
Inconsequential, as if
There were nothing to prove.

And though we may reflect
Upon their evident lack,
Dreams tell us of portals,
How we can never say
We are never coming back.

We cannot dream in the past.
In dreams we may not touch.
And though we are astounded,
Waking we often claim
That they were nothing much.

Oh, but they are fields of joy!
We ask for little more
When the cold world calls us,
Anchor drawn from the prow,
Stern slipping from the shore.

And I have nothing to give you
Except this love I send
In dreams of your own creating,
The life that has no body,
The story that has no end.

DREAMS

These peaceable hills have horses:
You hear them just across hedges,
Noses in interrogation
Nuzzling and nudging their foals.

Snorting and nodding the head
In the startled release of breath
That sends invisible plumes
To create a language of air.

Bolted down to their shadows,
Their muscles remember movement:
A shuddering of delight,
A flurry of tail and mane.

This field-family is guiltless
Of all romance and betrayal,
Of that conscious animal power
We exercise over each other.

And their unargumentative passion
Is simply the statement of life
That starts with a knock-kneed stagger,
The red badge of the birth-string.

Yet their labial hedge-sounds
Announce a familiar riddle
Which was spoken above our cradles
And haunts our every sleep.

It is always there unanswered,
As now, at dusk before dinner
When we take the garden steps
To the scurry and lisp of the Usk,

Trout-mothering river
But shallow over its stones
That speak an even more primal
Tongue of intense attention.

This half-light is a key
To the full knowledge of all
We attend to, all we intend
With our insistent questions.

The Men's Ward in moonlight
When one of two souls awake,
Trailing a bloody catheter,
Cries: 'Where's my wife, then?'

And his life that stands in the light,
The light that insists on the dark,
Holds both for a terrible moment
In a wailing sightless gaze,

As though a man in his pain
Must know where he casts his shadow
And why for an awkward season
He interrupts the light.

The moon mounts the mynydd
Needing nothing for itself,
Etching the tilted field
Like an expensive binding.

It needs nothing but its display:
The turrets above our pillow,
Our moments still together,
The scents, the long-lived river.

And the horses stand in the moon
As though what was always intended,
As though what was always meant,
Was to make their shadows new-minted.

They stand in the pitiless moon
As the sun stood over them,
And their noses stoop to the grass
Where their foals are at last asleep.

And so we, too, fall asleep,
Joining our mothers and fathers
In dreams, and in dreams of the dreams
That they must have dreamed before us.

THE BIRDS

At dusk the trees on the headland
Became a theatre for sparrows.

Leaves lifted and were after all wings
In simmering attendance

Rising and falling and rising
In silvery displacement.

We could imagine no peace
In that excited restless roosting

Rather a response to the moon
Which had lighted the lofty boughs

And left them in dim silhouette
As a place of argument and play,

A thousand fluttering occasions
Of exhaustion and dream.

The darkness acquired the intensity
Of mind at its moments of awareness,

Many leaves little darker than the sky
And the birds louder than water.

ROUND AND ROUND

New Year's Eve 1996: for Prue

I

Over and over, round and round
We tread a steady pulse, and out
Of sheer excitement, with a bound,
We ride again the roundabout
Of blood, and in bravado shout
Defiance at the turning sky
That turns about us till we die.

Over and over, walks discover
Things we are curious to see
As anecdotist, nature-lover,
Theorist of topography
(Or anything we care to be
While thus observing them). They link
Environment with how we think.

And royal stanzas turn these signs
In turn into a turning scene
Where light is scattered into lines
That lead the eye through what they mean,
Where they are headed, where they've been,
Turning over what they've found
Over and over, round and round.

It was the last walk of the year,
A unique vista from the tower
Which ordered days had built us here
(The walk well-known, well-timed, an hour
In length, taking in Hendre-Fawr,
The kilns of Cwm, the Quarry Lane
And Echo Valley, home again).

Gathering gorse-bits for the stove
Half-way round by Nant-y-cwm
(Roofless in a little grove
Of thorn and elder that makes room
For just one sheep-path in the gloom)
We stumbled on the frozen hill,
The clods and droppings hardened still.

For frost made splinters of the grass
And leaves lay crusted where they were.
Streams were silent veils of glass.
Nothing seemed likely to occur,
Nothing to cause the wind to stir,
Only the whiteness of the stones
And, in the brackened gullies, bones.

The bracken that was furred and furled
In summer now lay stiff and spilt:
The rusting corners of a world
That once was wiry, green and built
To last, the dry stems snapped and tilt-
ed like old gates adrift from hinges,
In brilliant tans, manilas, gingers.

There's a philosophy in walks
That circle round a point in view
Or take a turn (though no one talks)
About an ancient field or two,
Muse up and down, just me and you,
The mental mountain that is ours,
The valley of our idle hours.

It seemed surprising to be there,
Odd in a way to be alive,
As though we'd been allowed to share
The goats' decision to survive
(Twenty at most, as few as five

The last time that we counted them,
Each pair of horns a diadem).

Goats might be ghosts for all we know,
Leading a spiritual existence.
Certainly they go to show
That nature encourages persistence.
We know their profiles at a distance,
When beard and mountain say 'I am',
That small prophetic ideogram.

And though we hadn't seen them lately,
And we for our part seldom seen,
Less like Monkey Kings, less stately,
Sweeter-smelling, we had been
About the meanings that we mean
When thoughts make progress, all the while
Pacing their gradient, in file.

Embracing on those narrow shelves
Above the smoky maps of farms,
We felt like patriarchs ourselves,
Finding within each other's arms
A law worth silences for psalms,
Encoded in the dying form
That love has made and love keeps warm.

To follow on in single file
Is to obey the falling land
Which keeps the paths to threads. Meanwhile
My thoughts do likewise, single and
In sequence, not the hand-in-hand
Of systematic argument
Or a concerted clear intent.

A walk is like a life that turns
From outward expectation to

An inward recollection, learns
From what it has been made to do
How best to keep that motion true,
Like variations that redeem
In major chords their private theme.

How many have we taken now
That seemed to make a point of this?
Retracing purpose like a vow,
Closing the circle like a kiss
With that instinct analysis
That tells us, though we've lost the track,
We would get wetter turning back?

After Uwch-hafotty the path
Leads us as though it knows the way
Not to the heather but the hearth
(There are alternatives, but they
Are always for another day,
That mythic future of ambition
When habit yields to a decision).

And so we took the way of gates
That creak into the fields that lie
Straining above the tarry slates
Of Tan-y-bwlch to reach the sky,
The gates that once pleased ear and eye
By opening with latch and spring,
Now mostly looped with orange string.

Once, to enter was to pay
A visit. Shyness stayed outside
Until a garden showed the way
And working hands could win a bride.
Now gateposts show that someone died,
Empty of iron, or tied fast
As if to make that garden last.

Though there is nothing there to lead us
Beyond that asking gap except
A pair of wildered leaning cedars
And something like a stone where stepped
A polished boot, and a heart leaped,
Now there is only grass and fern,
The roots and stumps we take to burn.

Do we occasionally think
We see the glimmer of a face,
Blank at the window's gap, a blink?
Presiding absence in a place
Defined by absences? A space
That's its own echo? If we do,
Believing that we do's taboo.

We mustn't think that love survives.
These tales are tales of our own fear:
We last no longer than our lives,
Less long than crockery, which here
And there lies hidden with its clear
Blue stripes, its bridges and its swallows,
In twisty roots and bluebell hollows.

Below the cottage the ground drops
Through thorn and oak: could this have been
A garden once, this trickling copse?
The sheep inhabit it, half-seen,
This muddiness, this mezzanine
Where things undoubtedly occurred
And lip met lip, in kiss or word.

All silent now, save for the stirring
Of little waters and the ewes
Who stand in state or tread unerring
Like delegations, in tight shoes,
One of the two paths they might choose:

Up and away, adventurous
Like goats; or down and back, like us.

If in this silence roots were sounds,
If, in their tumbling, seeds made traces,
If we could break their deeps and bounds,
If we could plumb their hiding-places,
Flowers were promises and faces
And colours in the frozen ground,
For ever and ever, round and round.

Round we went, then, as a clock's
Hand comes back slowly even as
It scythes its path, or like a box
That while it slowly opens has
A spring that snaps it shut. It was
A walk in which the setting out
Defined the end it brought about.

Smoke from the cottage made a spire
That beaconed from a field away
Above the trees that fed its fire.
The teapot warmed to end the day,
And cake and cups filled up a tray.
Evening and pleasure were about,
And curtains kept the twilight out.

The stillness of the cottage was
The sort of stillness that's like thinking,
Which moves in quietness because
It must, but with a purpose, linking
The black mascara'd spider blinking
Along the wall in make-believe
With the next web it wants to weave.

Linked the wooden seagull with
The warm air from the stove that makes

It flap its wings towards its myth,
Some plywood shore where each wave breaks
On hinges; where at last it wakes
To a stiff ocean on which floats
A chubby fleet of painted boats.

Linked a blue cat to her dreams,
Linked the chimney to the wind
And windows to the night's extremes
Of temperature undisciplined
That would by morning leave them skinned
With frosty shapes as though the air
Had turned to ice and skated there.

Linked our eyes to everything
They saw, in fact, and no surprise
That seeing turned to happening
So that before our very eyes
Flames leaped within the stove, likewise
Within our hearts, as though our being
Depended somehow on that seeing.

Titles stirred upon the shelves
And ink became the proud inventor
Of words that recognised themselves,
Sapphire clicked and poised to enter
Between circumference and centre
The turning world of vinyl which
Sang out in passion at a switch.

2

Life is a drama well-attested.
In your sabbatical decade
You may feel wise and fully rested:
It's an illusion, I'm afraid.
Your world remains still to be made.

Playing at God, you scarcely could
Observe it and declare it good.

It's what from mountains you return to.
It is the commerce of the valleys.
It is the sultan's wish to learn to
Share with the outcasts in the alleys
(Or like the soul in Alfred's palace,
With culture surfeited, *distrait*,
Who went into the vale to pray).

Where have you ever found it, child
Of a decade of cold and hope?
Nothing is ever reconciled
And unfulfilled the horoscope.
Above the fire the envelope,
Propped with its slit, like a long fuse
Still contains depressing news.

It says we have to take our chance.
It says we cannot choose our parts.
It says time brings us to the dance.
It leads us, and it then departs
And will not finish what it starts
But leaves our little lives up-ended
And all our careful plans suspended.

We think there's something to bequeath,
Something worth chiselling in stone,
A monument to lie beneath
Of derring-do as yet unknown,
Something that we have made our own:
But when it comes to it, it all
Seems pallid and provisional.

We never tidied up our bedroom.
We voted but we did not strive

For social justice, gave no headroom
To our beliefs (conscripted half-alive
And put to work from nine to five).
We never learned consistency.
We oiled the lock but lost the key.

I crashed the gears. I hit the ditch.
I muffed the shot. I missed the red.
I lost the thread. I dropped a stitch.
I didn't hear what someone said
And said the other thing instead,
Or waited, furiously weak
And cross, for someone else to speak.

Truth stayed unopened on our shelves.
We toiled in certain fine pursuits
Yet spent the wages on ourselves.
The vineyard offered up its fruits
To auditors in three-piece suits.
We feared all those we loved because
We did not merit their applause.

We never listened, hardly spoke
More than delighted our own ears.
Half-asleep, we half-awoke
Then slept again, for years and years.
We breathed adjusted atmospheres,
Reclined on scatter-cushions with
Museum music for a myth.

We're used to being disenchanted.
We thought about the Welfare State
And then we took it all for granted.
We rushed to its defence too late
As though blind greed might fairly wait
Before annexing our resources
To the dead weight of market forces.

We should have known. It's an old story,
A sham that couldn't be much shammer.
It's rat-bites-terrier territory,
Whose selfishness is posed as glamour.
Politically, it's the hammer
Without the sickle, the whole nation
Unruly with deregulation.

Idealists turned self-righteous, throngs
Of creeps were put in charge, who crept.
We lost our rights and suffered wrongs
And all this happened while we slept
And let it happen, dazed, except
That nightmares fade when we awake.
This world is real, a real mistake.

Whatever we mistook for health
We picked up in the marketplace.
We looked for bargains, found ill-wealth,
The kind that drains the public face
But pulses in some private place.
Though irritating, it's the rich
Who show you where to scratch the itch.

In city streets the dusty elms
Are pollarded like amputees;
The dying sunset overwhelms
The window-panes with prodigies
Of heavenly telegraphese;
Perched on a saddle like a skull,
A small boy bucks his bicycle.

Rich in differentiation,
This is the sexual city where
Lit windows glow in isolation
Above each darkening railinged square
Where in our studenthood, aware

Of otherness, we learned forbearance
And had to meet each other's parents.

In private while we learned to kiss,
In public we turned up for meals
And tested every prejudice
Of family in such ordeals
By learning what a mother feels
(The more possessive, mine, by far,
But yours the one with the cigar).

And after all, ours was true feeling:
Your attic room in Islington
Was papered over walls and ceiling
With flowers that rarely saw the sun.
Rooftop intruders, one by one,
Were in your fearful dreams cut down
By the foil beneath your eiderdown.

Now you were finally befriended
By one who could not let you go.
Your independent childhood ended
When we together went below,
Conscious beneath the portico
Of something like a destiny
That left us both no longer free.

Free, though, to each other and
The world we have neglected. Would
We have the wit to understand
These failures better if we stood
Alone and so against them? Could
Our long contentment hide the sting
Of our ignoring everything?

It is too late to answer this
With credibility, too late

For serious analysis,
Too late to do much more than wait
And watch and circumambulate
In celebration of contriving
Sixty whole years of mere surviving.

And most of those with you: they make
A claim against the void that waits
With pure indifference to take
Our bodies from us. That is fate's
Grim pleasure, naturally, which dates
Our deaths precisely. But who cares?
We gave that substance to our heirs.

I know we wouldn't wish life shorter,
Though longing wouldn't make it last.
Once it had doubled to a daughter
We knew that this might happen fast,
Our future mostly turn to past.
But now that so much past has been
Achieved, the present is serene.

Yes, we are not ourselves exactly:
Our daughters take us further than
Our natural scope, matter-of-factly,
The plain fulfilment of a plan
That we had sketched when we began,
Not knowing what we did, of course,
No inkling of that tour-de-force.

Now that we've seen our feelings scatter,
Now that we can let them go,
It's you three, surely, who now matter,
You who are growing still, although
We are the ground from which you grow,
The mulch, the furrow, the terrain,
The soil that will not yield again.

Take what you will of us, the steady
Spooling out is a release.
It has delivered us already.
It is your gift. It is our peace.
It is your life, and our decease.
It is our love we say good-bye with.
It is your love that we will die with.

3

Now from the confident perspective
Of almost forty years I look
Back in a mood that's part reflective,
Part quizzical, as in a book
Of photographs that someone took
For fun but somehow never showed me.
This is the view that memory owed me.

First I remember a green room
With sloping floor, and balcony
From which I heard the tower's boom
And timely cadence quarterly
Issuing with authority
And lifted melancholy tone
Out of that faceless clock of stone.

You in your duffle coat as grey
As frost, and cheek almost as cold,
I with my heart in disarray:
These searching moments are soon told
Although they last for ever, old
In telling and for what they mean
To those who acted in the scene.

I thought you as possessed of your
Own life as music is that eats
The air up like a meteor

And fills it with pure sound, repeats
And varies its effects with feats
Of effortless involved refrain,
And then is silent once again.

Those bells were soon eclipsed and you
Were quiet and hidden in your hair
From which your thinking eyes looked through
At mine that wished to join you there,
As in a private garden where
Concentric paths were unexplored
And wandering is its own reward.

Touch has no equal eloquence,
For sight is dumb with what it sees
And yet in touch each other sense
Learns soon enough that they may please
By serving it, as indices
Of its long-undisputed worth,
As doctors that must give it birth.

That coat! Inestimable garment,
Whose pockets held your hands before
I dared to, fearing my disbarment:
It was the grey of stone, and more –
The grey of thinking deeply or
Of pilgrimage or, I suppose,
The grey of Moyakeska's nose.

Half-open, it was like a book
Recording everything that we'd
Not yet begun to do. I took
Its pages and began to read
And found my future there indeed
In all that it so plainly clothed,
To which I surely was betrothed.

Lips shape passion's signifiers
With breath that is their subject; lips
When doing this are never liars
For their attentiveness equips
The journeys of relationships
With words to climb down precipices
And rations of long-lasting kisses.

To live by words and not to know
Their force! To struggle in the dumb
Undifferentiated flow
Of feelings, like the martyrdom
Of screaming in a vacuum
With someone smiling very near
And very dear, who cannot hear.

Bad dreams indeed. We misbehave
Out of mere weakness, failing still
To speak the only words that save,
Learning to live without our will,
Finding no projects to fulfil,
No moment when a certain vision
Lights up our firmly-made decision.

So, like a music that enlarges
Towards an ending it will greet
Without resentment, life discharges
The obligations it must meet
To be in the fullest sense complete:
This is its grandeur and its debt,
A gift that saves us from regret.

So we set out, if not with patience
Then with a certain certainty
That lent those various occasions
When I or you took you or me
In careless relativity

Too much for granted, a sad sense
Of criminal incompetence.

How easy, this ability
To lose whatever we possess
By ceasing to believe that we
Deserve such brilliant success.
We challenge it, we re-assess
The circumstances that gave rise
To being given such a prize.

And then we throw it all away
Simply by wanting something new,
Something that's different, we say,
But nothing different will do.
The vision doesn't stop being true
For passing into legend, nor
Can meaning live outside the law.

The music that we played exchanged
My kind of lyric line with yours.
Your taste in vocalising ranged
From Bizet's absolute amours
To Greco's or Charles Aznavour's;
I liked the grunting of Stan Getz,
Or Shostakovitch's quartets.

Sibelius's Violin
Concerto was our haunting ground:
Beneath the violinist's chin
As the LP went crackling round
An icy and exquisite sound
Was slowly launched. On that first movement
I could imagine no improvement.

It was as music is, not source
But symbol of a new emotion

Which, even as it took its course
Excitedly upon an ocean
Of high adventure and devotion,
Was reckless of geography
Or navigation, you or me.

Sitting with biscuits on the rug,
I needed to be more than guest.
The coffee in your Spanish mug
Cooled as the double-stops suppressed
All talk, all casual interest
In what the two of us were saying
Before the music started playing.

Drifting, I had run aground.
Caught in your arms I was released.
Lost in your aura, I was found.
Your West fulfilled my searching East,
My spirit and my sacred beast,
My moon, my many and my one,
My conscience and my sense of fun.

Such rooms, all rooms, where we can be
Ourselves, together or alone,
Are like our life itself that we
Inhabit and can call our own,
Free space to which we've slowly grown,
A private exhibition for
Ourselves, but with an open door.

4

At midnight, then, we climbed the hill
With whisky and a lantern's glow
Which lit the stone it stood on till
The shadows made it monstrous, so
That lighted scatterings of snow

About it seemed to celebrate
In dance the dying of the date.

Each flake that flew into its beam
Was strangely lifted in the light,
Turned like a jewel, made to seem
Unfalling in our searching sight
Though quickly swallowed by the night
That occupied the air about us
And would have been content without us.

The year was like the earth it passed,
Changed yet unchanging to the sense
That closely watched it. As the last
Was once the next, mere accidence
Of time, performance changed in tense
And not in any substance, so
There was no death for it to owe.

We filled our glasses and we reckoned
That minute's round till it was done,
Counted each andante second
One by one by one by one.
Sixty there were at first, then none:
We counted one to fifty-nine
For every birthday that was mine.

In that suspended second, when
The moment came for vows, we vowed.
My watch displayed four noughts and then
We spoke our wishes out aloud.
As if to ratify them, cloud
Dissolved unseen above the hill
Revealing Orion, belted, still.

And, ah, those stars! Cold fixity
Making their shapes for ever, though

Especially for me at sixty,
As if to say: 'Blow, winds, blow
And crack your cheeks', and then to show
Themselves as puzzles, calendars,
Heroic stridings, those nude stars!

It was a moment of great love.
We downed the whisky and we stood
Upon the earth it tasted of,
Belonging to it while we could
And looking beyond Elernion Wood
Across the bay to Anglesey
Where flashes of fire lit up the sea.

The stars are like the spines of books
We think we're going to read one day.
They are the shining eyes and hooks
Of night, the grand couturier
Who sweeps the sky in disarray,
Stirring the frosty crowns of trees
That glitter in their symmetries.

Now my days are well-begun.
The number of the days I'd seen?
I added up to twenty-one
Thousand nine hundred and fifteen.
I felt it worthwhile having been
In all those daily hiding-places,
So many fruitful solar spaces.

Spaces that are global births,
Spaces around me as I write
Shaped by the ancient restless earth's
Impulsive turning from the night
To bask again in open light,
Spaces that we fill with news
Like blanks for which we have no clues.

Days are an ad hoc inventory,
Deeds to the house of life, unknown
Until unearthed, the territory
That we must try to map, alone.
Days are everything we own,
Successive shapes not quite the same.
Each is what the next became.

And what the last had hoped to be,
Gone when delivered, named and lost,
Leaves fallen from a single tree
That keep their shape as long as frost
Preserves them, veins embossed
With crystals on a fading brown,
Dead days for ever falling down.

Still cold. The wind got underneath
Our eyelids and the lantern guttered.
But no, it wasn't like Lear's heath
When those defiant words he uttered
Were those that anyone has muttered
Who has destroyed but not rebuilt
A world subtended from his guilt.

We felt instead the vigour and
The new resolve inherent in
The moment, like the borderland
Of questing country, discipline
That has for patient ages been
The stoic assumption of our neighbours,
Their life of waiting and of labours.

So the day's cycle ended, and
The year's, and it was time to go
Down to the cottage, hand in hand,
From which, as usual, just below,
It sent its civilising glow

From one small pane, a tidy light
That focused, and required, the night.

Down to the warmth, the banked-up coal
That made our tiny windows weep,
Down, and then up to bed, the soul
Entering at last the deep
Black pages of the book of sleep
In which our voyaging dreams are bound
Over and over, round and round.

THREE FOR PRUE

1 A Boy Writing

This solemn shrimp, poring over his slate,
Is as naked as the hope he embodies.

One knee is lifted to support the careful capitals,
As if he is ready to leap up from his stool in joy.

But for the moment he is caught in alabaster,
In a lucidity of concentration.

Writing gets no more serious than this,
The first slow act, the letters about to shout aloud.

And you, my dearest, who have the knowledge
At the very heart of you, often near breaking it,

You must know that this little putto has a meaning
For you alone, for all you have achieved

For children whose similar beauty is only damaged
By the slightest crack in the smoothness of the marble

And whose own exclamations of gratitude and joy
Are as eternal as sculpture, and as silent.

2 Two Kites

Yours is a ruffled red bird,
Mine a staring green eye and a tail.

You ride the wind and sing,
I sidle and weave.

Where did we come from
Before we went aloft, adventuring?

We had been cared for by a few who had known
The simpler energies of horses and candles.

Is this why we search for such elemental things?
Here we are; and there we were.

The world's a wild place.
We reach out as we can.

Weak struts, papery ribbons, a drum of thread,
And the hope of an afternoon of air.

The strings hum, unreeled from the chest.
When they cross, it is mine that snaps

Who cares who goes first, the sky so blue?
It is the humming, and the tug.

Your kite is steady above us.
Its flying shadow darkens the field.

The grass flickers at its passing.
The grass darkens and burns

3 Primroses

An anonymous archangel called in to say
That the primroses we picked will last another day.

How many times have we bunched the stems,
Cradling the heads in a single leaf of their kind?

How many such small crowds of flowers
Have looked over their green glazed rim

As if to wonder what sort of a space they were in,
Blankly, as their yellow pales into cream

And the green at the centre is a forgotten dream,
An echo of that cold season before growing?

You who have been called to a great exploit of rescue,
To raise the flower on its broken stem

Know that this business of caring is the need
To restore an elemental touch.

These are like all your assisted children,
Who would certainly crowd if they could

With a similar reach and twist of the head
To smile their sweetest smiles for you.

Gathered by you along the winding hedges of your life,
Noticed particularly in their own shorter journey.

Sweetness out of ditches, cardigan smells,
Granny's smell, Edie's smell, the sweetness of memory.

Sweetness in your loose fist, the sweetness
Of following you down this ancient lane for ever.

PROLOGUE AND EPILOGUE

Those twenty years we lived before we met,
Long gone yet partly traced, like history,
Seem now discountable, mysterious,
Petty to be regretted as not shared,
As two paths through a thicket reach the same
Broad upland meadow with its untrod grasses
A feathery haze of red, a Corot trick
To lose the single tuft among its kind
And lead the eye to wander where the light
Has only brilliant remarks to make.

And if my own path was a thorny stumble,
Grateful to find an opening at last,
I hardly cared what opportunities
You'd had to choose between alternatives
Or where those led, or if it mattered to you.
The seeds have fallen now, the grass is flattened,
We've almost done our feasting in the sun.
Together we attend the earliest star
As to a strict instructor of our fate,
And know by now how to respect its tale.

It stands there in the evening sky, as always
Suggesting endings and continuations,
A point of closure that allows the next
Inevitable sentence to begin,
A single blast that notifies the squadrons,
The brooding horn that wakes concerted strings,
The constellations waiting for their darkness,
The heavens waiting for the world to sleep
And we to watch, as one by one the stars
Shape their cold oracles at our request.

The future and the past might well be here
If we could read them as they once were read
Two thousand years ago on terraces
Like this, in villas very much the same
Beside this restless, many-harboured sea.
And still we give them that ironic look
Which tries to make them somehow, in our vast
Belittlement, accomplices of sorts.
We introduce them, like the years themselves,
Into our shapely private narrative.

But always underneath there is this murmur
Of some lost language, almost translatable
Yet fraught with meanings never caught or shared,
Those random busy years our life escaped from,
The years I still can be resentful of,
Remembering the unrememberable,
And finding them as chastening in their way
As what we neither of us know, their final
Counterpart, the matching epilogue,
The twenty years we hope we still have left.

If history has always been like this,
Shaped only by our accidental myths
And flowing anywhere (as Hardy put it:
A roadside rill after a thunderstorm,
Turned by a straw, or tiny bar of sand)
Then should we care what shape our water takes?
Where it has come from? Where it thinks it goes?
Its greatest moments, and the most surprising,
Are what we dare to give the name of love,
The meeting of our tributary streams.